Katherine Swynford

KATHERINE SWYNFORD

Anthony Goodman

The Honywood Press
Lincoln Cathedral Publications
1994

Published 1994 by
The Honywood Press
Lincoln Cathedral Library
Lincoln LN2 1PZ

Reprinted 1999, 2001, 2004, 2006

ISBN 1 870561 07 4

Cover design by Ruddocks Design & Print, Lincoln
Illustrations by David Vale
Printed by Ruddocks Design & Print, Lincoln

Cataloguing-in-Publication Data
	**A catalogue entry for this publication is available from the
	British Library**

ACKNOWLEDGMENTS

I owe thanks for advice and encouragement in writing this pamphlet to Dr Nicholas Bennett, Dr Alison McHardy, Canon John Nurser and Dr Dorothy Owen.

Anthony Goodman
February 1993

KATHERINE SWYNFORD

Katherine Swynford is one of the most famous, enigmatic and controversial of medieval women. Born presumably c. 1350, she was a daughter of Payn de Roet, a knight from Hainault, which was then an independent principality in the Holy Roman Empire and is now part of Belgium. Roet was one of the many Hainaulters who came to England to seek the patronage of Queen Philippa (d. 1369), a member of the ruling family of Hainault, and of her husband Edward III (d. 1377), one of medieval England's great warrior-kings. Roet's expertise in the 'laws of arms' (the conventions of chivalrous warfare) impressed King Edward, who appointed him as one of his chief heralds, 'Gujenne King of Arms.[1]

By the 1360s Roet had succeeded in pladng both Katherine and her sister Philippa in offices in princely households and in marrying them to up-and-coming young Englishmen. In 1366 Philippa was the wife of Geoffrey Chaucer, one of the king's esquires: in that year she was granted an annuity of 10 marks for her office as a lady in the queen's chamber.[2] Before then Katherine had married a Lincoinshire knight, Hugh Swynford, who had entered on his inheritance in 1361.[3] Katherine too became a lady-in-waiting, to a great heiress, Blanche of Lancaster. In 1359 Blanche had been the bride of one of Edward III's sons, John of Gaunt (1340-1399). So named because of his birth in Ghent, this sturdy, personable and dutiful prince, who had a keen eye for feminine charms, was eager to emulate the chivalrous achievements of the renowned elder brother who had helped to educate him: Edward Prince of Wales (1330-1376), known to posterity as the Black Prince. John of Gaunt gained the material basis for high military command when in 1362 he acquired, in right of his wife, the whole of the Lancastrian inheritance, so becoming, as duke of Lancaster, the possessor of the largest collection of noble landed estates in England, with lordships in Wales and France as well. The evidence suggests that he mourned deeply when Blanche died in 1368, at about the age of 22. A year or so earlier she had given birth at Bolingbroke Castle (Lincolnshire) to their only son, the future King Henry IV (reigned 1399-1413), the first ruler of the Lancastrian dynasty. A genuine sense of loss shines through the conventional courtly verses in which Blanche's untimely death was mourned by Geoffrey Chaucer, in *The Boke of the Duchesse* and, more movingly, by the chronicler Jean Froissart in *Le Joli Buisson de Jonece*.

In the decade after Blanche's death, Gaunt's career took off, though without entirely happy consequences. He became a leading player in international politics and the most influential subject in England. In 1371 he remarried: his bride was a Spanish princess, Constance, the beautiful, devout and tragic daughter and heiress of Pedro I of Castile, 'Pedro the Cruel'. Her father had recently been brutally murdered by his own half-brother, Enrique of Trastamara, who usurped the throne. Constance fled to English protection: in 1372 Gaunt laid claim to the Crown of Castile in her right. Over the next few years the physical decline of the Black Prince, now an invalid, and of the ageing Edward III, and then the accession to the throne in 1377 of the Prince's ten-year-old son Richard II thrust Gaunt into the political limelight as the senior active male in the royal family. In the last year or so of Edward's reign and the first four years of Richard's minority, Gaunt's maladroit handling at crucial points of the Commons in parliament, the English Church and the City of London, together with reverses in the warfare with the French Crown and its Castilian allies, which resumed in 1377, made him widely unpopular.

Coincidentally, the fact that Katherine had become the duke's mistress became public knowledge and a subject of scandalised gossip. The duke's harshest critic amongst contemporary chroniclers, Thomas Walsingham, monk of St Alban's Abbey (Hertfordshire), used the liaison with Katherine as a stick with which to belabour him. Under the year 1378, Walsingham denounced Gaunt for brazenly touring the country with his mistress to the neglect of his military responsibilities, and for humiliating the Duchess Constance.

Another chronicler, Henry Knighton, canon of Leicester Abbey, was particularly well informed about happenings in the ducal household, since members of it frequently visited Gaunt's castle at Leicester.

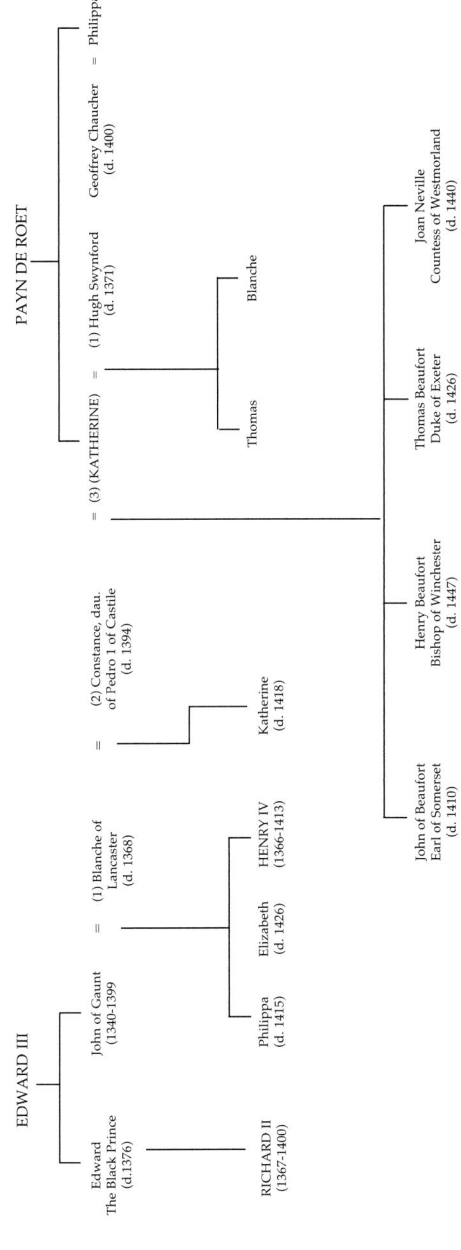

A simplified geneological table showing the families of John of Gaunt and Katherine Swynford

9

Knighton, habitually reverential in his references to the 'pious duke' (who was his abbey's patron) sorrowfully recalled how the latter had been repeatedly told by clerics and by his own domestic servants of the bad effects on his reputation of his suspiciously close relations with Katherine.[5] Her usurpation of the duchess's rightful place in Lancastrian affairs is graphically reflected by entries in the records of the duke's borough of Leicester. Under the year 1375-6 it was noted that the mayor had sent Katherine some wine, and, under 1377-9, presents of a horse and an iron pan, the latter in gratitude for her success in expediting a property matter for the borough and for procuring its exemption from a loan to the Crown.[6]

However, the 'bad press' which Katherine received was not to create a malignant image of her in later historical writings. Her memory was on the whole respected, because Gaunt eventually married her and procured the legitimation of their children, who had been given the surname of Beaufort. The Beaufort family played leading political and dynastic roles in fifteenth-century England. The Lancastrian kings, who ruled from 1399 to 1461, regarded them as trusted kinsfolk. Cicely, duchess of York, mother of the Lancastrians' successors, the Yorkist kings Edward IV (d. 1483) and Richard III (d. 1485), was a grand-daughter of Katherine. More crucially, the right to the throne of the Tudor monarchs (reigned 1485-1603), resting on their descent from John of Gaunt, came through the Beaufort line. The first Tudor king, Henry VII, was the son of Lady Margaret Beaufort, whose spotlessly pious reputation contrasted markedly with that of her wayward great-grandmother, Katherine Swynford.

KATHERINE'S LIFE AND CAREER
Katherine was the wife of Hugh Swynford and a member of Blanche of Lancaster's household by 24 January 1365, when Bishop Buckingham of Lincoln referred to her as the duchess's *ancille* (female servant) in a privilege which he granted to her: she was permitted to have divine service celebrated privately (that is, in her household, perhaps in an oratory adjoining her chamber) up to the time of Pentecost, whenever she visited Leicester - which was likely to be frequently, because of the Lancastrian residence there.[7] Sir Hugh

Swynford died in November 1371, overseas - presumably in south-west France, where he had probably been serving Gaunt; perhaps he was a casualty of warfare with the French. Hugh left a little boy as heir - his son Thomas, born in 1367 or 1368.[8] There was also a daughter, Blanche, to whom Gaunt stood godfather: her name suggests that she was born before Thomas, and had the duchess as her godmother.[9]

Katherine, in her widowhood, held (possibly from 1372 onwards) an important post in the Lancastrian household: in 1376 Gaunt granted her the wardship and marriage of a minor as a reward for the 'good and agreeable' service which she had performed as governess of Duchess Blanche's daughters Philippa and Elizabeth, an office which she was to hold till 1381.[10] Since Katherine's office entailed periods of residence in the ducal household, it provided cover for her assignations with Gaunt. When the prince and the governess became lovers is unclear. They later solemnly declared that it was when Gaunt was married to Constance of Castile and Katherine was a widow.[11] However, the chronicler Froissart, who picked up a lot of courtiers' gossip, asserted, also many years later, that they were lovers during Hugh Swynford's lifetime.[12] In Hainault in 1411, perhaps as a result of Froissart's assertion, doubts were raised about the true paternity of her son Thomas.[13] Gaunt's modern biographer Sydney Armitage-Smith tentatively dated the births of their children, the Beauforts, to 1373, 1375, 1377 and 1379.[14] Circumstantial evidence suggests that the affair started in 1372, corroborating the couple's testimony. For Gaunt was out of England, campaigning and governing in south-west France, from the summer of 1370 until his return in November 1371 with his bride Constance. It is unlikely that Katherine would have accompanied her husband to France with Gaunt's military retinue. In the years after Gaunt's return he was to bestow a lavish stream of favours and rewards on Katherine which, cumulatively, were more than was appropriate for the widow of a knight who had died in his service and the governess of two of his daughters.[15] The first grant, made on 15 May 1372, was a life annuity of 50 marks, which more than doubled the annuities which Katherine received for her past service to Blanche.[16] In June 1373, at his army headquarters at

Northbourne (Kent) on the eve of invading France, Gaunt was thinking about Katherine's well-being as well as his wife's during his absence on campaign, ordering the delivery to Katherine of venison, fuel for the winter and oaks for building material, and enjoining that her annuity was to be paid to her 'without any kind of excuse'.[17] He made an unusual grant in 1375: a reward of an annuity of five marks for life to a widow, Agnes Bonsergeant, for the services which she had performed for Katherine when she was her nurse.[18] It was usual for princes and nobles in adulthood to recall and provide favourably for their own wet-nurses: for one to do so for an unrelated lady's wet-nurse was eccentric and, surely, a sign of great affection for the lady. In 1380 or 1381 Gaunt gave Katherine a highly personal and cosily domestic gift - a silver chafing-pan (*chaufour*), which had three feet and a handle and was supplied to Gaunt by one of his customary purveyors of luxury goods, Herman, goldsmith of London.[19]

The reason why the children of Gaunt and Katherine were given the surname 'Beaufort' is a mystery: no contemporary or fifteenth-century source provides an explanation. A clue is perhaps to be found in the evidence provided in 1400 by witnesses at an inquisition to determine whether a certain Roger Deincourt, son of Sir John, was of age. Their evidence was that he was born in 1377 at Kenilworth Castle (Gaunt's magnificent Warwickshire residence) and baptised there and that his godfather was the pope's brother Roger Beaufort, Gaunt's prisoner in the castle, in the custody of the baby's father.[20] Their memories are credible: Roger Beaufort, a member of a distinguished southern French family, was the brother of Pope Gregory XI (d. 1378), with whom Gaunt had close diplomatic relations; Roger had been captured by the English in 1370. Gaunt was therefore 'master' to a distinguished prisoner, with whom his relations are likely to have been cordial as well as of great political importance. It may have been as a mutual compliment between Gaunt and Beaufort that the former's children were given this honourable family name. Perhaps, too, it was an attempt to disguise their paternity.

The flawed romantic idyll was broken by the terrors of the Peasants' Revolt in 1381. Gaunt was the principal 'traitor' denounced by the rebellious rustics of Kent and Essex, who stunned the king and

Kettlethorpe Hall: the fourteenth~entury gateway

nobles when they streamed through the defences of London, welcomed and cheered on by the common folk of the city. Anyone connected with Gaunt rightly felt in deadly peril, in London and elsewhere. His teenage son, Henry of Bolingbroke, narrowly escaped death in the Tower of London when the rebels took it over; a friar was beheaded on Tower Hill simply because he was Gaunt's physician. Luckily for the duke, he was in the Anglo-Scottish borders, negotiating a truce, when the Revolt broke out: he was able to take refuge with the sympathetic Scots. Katherine (and Constance) he left abandoned in England: Katherine 'went into hiding where no one knew where to find her for a long time'. Dismissing his servants before setting off into exile, Gaunt declared that

> he supposed that God wished to chastise him for his misdeeds and the evil life which he had for long led, namely in the sin of lechery, in which he had 'particularly associated with dame Katherine de Swynford, a she-devil and enchantress, and with many others in his wife's household, against the will of God and the law of holy church.[21]

English chroniclers were deeply, and favourably, impressed by Gaunt's public displays of remorse - even his most virulent critic, Walsingham; they gave his repentance 'front page' treatment. During his brief exile at Holyrood Abbey, Edinburgh, Gaunt again made his feelings clear - the English were probably horrified at the thought of humbling oneself amidst the Scots! The chronicler Knighton says that the duke promised to expel Katherine from his household and that he did so after his return to England. This was in July 1381, about three weeks after his flight, and in the dying days of the Revolt. On the way south, at Northallerton, Gaunt met his duchess, who had also had a nerve wracking time. Raising Constance's prostrate figure from the ground, he commiserated with her, and she with him: he kissed her and gently asked her pardon for his misconduct. 'She forgave him willingly and there was great joy and celebration between them and with their companions'.[22] After this affecting scene, echoing in the monastic chronicler's description the conventions of courtly romance, it is not surprising that Gaunt did indeed distance himself from Katherine. A few months later he granted her the enormous life annuity of 200 marks for her good service to his daughters - which sounds like a pay-off.[23] In February 1382 Katherine was referred to as his daughters' former governess.[24]

Gaunt's resolution was reinforced in the mid-1380s by changes in political circumstances which favoured his claim to the Crown of Castile: Froissart depicts him as relying heavily on Constance's counsel in the matter and in June 1386 the pair sailed with an army to Castile in pursuit of the throne. It was not until November 1389 that Gaunt sailed back to England from Gascony. However, in the meantime Katherine was not cut off from all contact with Gaunt and the Lancastrian milieu. In 1386 or 1387 Gaunt ordered the payment to her of £100, part of a loan of 500 marks which she had lent him 'in his great necessity'.[25] Henry of Bolingbroke's wife Mary gave Katherine and her daughter Joan Beaufort presents for New Year 1388.[26] Meanwhile, the renewed bonds between Gaunt and Constance sagged as the fulfilment of their Castilian ambitions faded in the privations of a disastrous summer campaign in Leon in 1387. After the couple gave up their claims to the Crown of Castile in 1388, Constance lost her political importance to Gaunt. Within a few years of Gaunt's return to England in 1389, Katherine is found staying again in his household.[27] Constance's death in 1394 enabled him to take steps towards the legitimation of his Beaufort children, though these had to wait until after a year's visit by him to Gascony. Within weeks of returning, Gaunt retired from the King's court and travelled to Lincoln, where Katherine was staying: there they married on 14 January 1396. This misalliance provoked universal amazement, according to Walsingham.[28] Froissart says that aristocratic ladies, such as Gaunt's devout sister-in-law Eleanor, duchess of Gloucester, and the countess of Arundel, declared that the duke had disgraced himself by marrying his mistress and that their hearts would burst with grief if they had to allow her precedence.[29] They soon had to swallow their pride. Duchess Katherine, in accordance with her status, played a leading part in the ceremonies at and around Richard II's town of Calais later that year, when the king married Isabella, the seven-year-old daughter of Charles VI of France. Gaunt and Katherine were to entertain the queen in their London house - probably when Gaunt was renting Ely Place in Holborn, whose fine medieval chapel and its undercroft still continue in ecclesiastical use. On this occasion Gaunt presented Isabella with a great cup and bowl of gold; Katherine gave her a cup of more manageable size for a little girl.[30]

It is an indication that Gaunt's marriage was a middle-aged love-match, not just a device to legitimise his children, that he was not content to envisage that, if widowed, Katherine would have only dower of the Lancastrian inheritance: in 1397 he arranged that parts of it would be held jointly for their lives.[31] However, the brief three years of Katherine's second marriage were to be clouded, not only by the growing political tensions which were to culminate in Henry of Bolingbroke's exile in 1398 and Richard II's deposition at his hands in 1399, but by Gaunt's recurrent bouts of sickness, which sometimes prevented him from travelling. In February 1398, at the end of a parliamentary session at Shrewsbury, he was too ill to travel far and, with Katherine in his company, convalesced at Lilleshall Abbey. In the will which he made that month, he included lavish bequests for her, such as all the jewels he kept in a little coffer, his best badge of Richard II's livery (the emblem of the white hart) with its fine ruby, and his best collar (presumably his device of the esses) lavishly set with diamonds. Gaunt's health finally deteriorated the following winter and he died in Leicester Castle on 3 February 1399. In his deathbed agony, if a fifteenth-century tradition is to be believed, he attributed his bodily ills (as he had his political ones in 1381) to lecherous behaviour - if so, a further cause of distress to Katherine. With her son Henry Beaufort, bishop of Lincoln, she accompanied the cortège southwards towards London, through Dunstable, St Albans and Barnet. Presumably she was present in London for the exequies, first at the Whitefriars, fleet Street, then in the place of interment, the choir of St Paul's Cathedral. There Gaunt was laid to rest beside the body of Duchess Blanche in the magnificent chantry chapel he had long ago had built for her and for himself. The chapel, with its stone effigies of the pair, and the duke's lance and shield hanging near his tomb, were a prominent feature of the cathedral until consumed in the Great Fire of London in 1666.

Soon after Gaunt's death, Richard II confiscated his inheritance, to prevent his exiled son Henry from inheriting it - a move which was to bring about Richard's downfall. However, he showed due consideration to Katherine, allowing her to have her jointure and later granting her petition asking to receive back her own properties which, she said, had been wrongfully seized by royal officials along with Gaunt's.[32] Nevertheless, despite Richard's good treatment of her, it was doubtless a relief when her 'son' Henry of Bolingbroke held the Crown. Katherine died on 10 May 1403, according to the inscription which was once on her tomb.[33]

KATHERINE'S REPUTATION

How did Katherine's contemporaries view her? To what extent did her behaviour flout conventional morality and hierarchical propriety? It was quite usual for bereaved young ladies to opt for a life of widowhood, avoiding the renewed subjection of marriage and the hazards of childbirth. Some lived in conspicuous piety, often having taken public oaths of lifelong chastity. Others took a lover, as did Henry V's flighty widow Katherine of Valois (her beloved being Katherine Swynford's grandson, Edmund Beaufort). Katherine Swynford offended convention by her lack of discretion, not by taking an exalted lover. It was normal for kings and nobles to have mistresses of inferior status and to recognise and provide for their illegitimate children, as did Edward III and the Black Prince. For Katherine, the timing of her liaison was unfortunate. Some of Gaunt's growing unpopularity in the 1370s rubbed off on her. At a time of national

The tombs of Katherine Swynford and her daughter Joan
in Lincoln Cathedral

crisis, contemporaries believed that, to God's displeasure and the jeopardy of the English nation, a lecherous woman, foreign in origin, was leading astray the prince upon whose suspect and wavering rectitude the king and the realm heavily depended. Yet she was not widely nor lastingly hated. She was not denounced with the same intensity as Alice Perrers, the undoubtedly grasping and corrupt mistress of Edward III's declining years. Gaunt, when politically ascendant, did not make the mistake of rewarding Katherine conspicuously at the Crown's expense.

Katherine won the respect of the leading contemporary pundit on correct courtly behaviour - the chronicler (and cleric) Jean Froissart who was, however, naturally prejudiced in her favour, since he, like her father, came from Hainault. He justly remarked, apropos the scandal of her marriage to Gaunt, that she was well suited to be a duchess, since she had been brought up since her youth in princely courts. Indeed, Gaunt would only have appointed as governess to two of his daughters a lady of serious demeanour, who possessed a well-informed piety and a knowledge of romantic literature and household economy, as well as a delight and aptitude in the more frivolous courtly accomplishments and games. Katherine's elder charge, Philippa of Lancaster (d. 1415) was to do her credit. Philippa, as the queen of João I of Portugal, won golden opinions in her adopted country for her wifely devotion and the good liturgical order kept in her household. However, Elizabeth, the younger daughter in Katherine's tutelage, soon went astray, causing a great scandal within a few years of being out of Katherine's charge. A headstrong teenager nominally married to a little boy who was heir to the earldom of Pembroke, Elizabeth destroyed a dynastic union important to her father through her seduction by Richard II's dashing and dangerous half-brother Sir John Holand, to whom she was consequently married.

How was Katherine regarded in Lancastrian circles? Leaving aside the sexual magnetism to which that experienced seducer, Gaunt, bore rueful testimony, she had an attractive personality, earning affection and respect, both as a girl and as a mature woman with a dubious past. Gaunt noted that the life annuity she received from her service to the Duchess Blanche had been doubled because of the 'great affection' which the duchess bore towards her.[34] Gaunt's son and heir Henry of Bolingbroke, in the 1390s a companion in chivalrous pursuits of her sons John and Thomas Beaufort, sent her fine New Year's presents.[35] Soon after Bolingbroke's accession in 1399 as Henry IV, he provided for the household needs of the 'king's mother' by an annual grant to her for life of four barrels of wine.[36]

However, Katherine's dubious role in the ducal household in the 1370s could not but provoke domestic tensions. She threatened harmony in Lancastrian circles by receiving outstanding and doubtless coveted material favours from the duke and by providing an improper alternative channel of favour for suitors who ought rather to have petitioned the duchess. She undermined the responsibility which the duke bore as the head of a household to oversee the morals of his (mostly male) servants - a responsibility which his saintly great-grandson, Henry VI, discharged by spying through peepholes on any woman entering his house, lest what he piously regarded as their innate foolishness might lead his servants into sin.

Echoes of division and disquiet over Katherine may be faintly signalled in two passages written by her highly discreet brother-in-law, Geoffrey Chaucer, in *The Canterbury Tales*. One might have expected that this London vintner's son would have applauded her relationship with a king's son, which was to bring his descendants within the circle of the royal kinsfolk. However, in *The Phisiciens Tale* Chaucer refers apologetically but caustically to governesses with a dubious past. His exhortations cannot but bring Katherine's case to mind.[37] In *The Monkes Tale* Chaucer has a panegyric on Constance's father, King Pedro of Castile, and a lament for the treacherous assassination which he suffered.[38] However, Pedro's memory was almost certainly held in ill-disguised contempt by Gaunt and his English knights who had once campaigned in Spain to restore the Castilian king. Briefly re-enthroned, Pedro had appeared faithless and ungrateful in the eyes of his saviours, the Black Prince and Gaunt. Chaucer here seems to write as a partisan of Duchess Constance, for she reverenced the memory of her ferocious father. Perhaps the poet was recollecting the views of his deceased wife Philippa. After Constance's arrival as Gaunt's bride in England in 1371, Philippa, as a lady-in-waiting, was one of Constance's confidantes from about the time of her first pregnancy - an embarrassing post, one might conclude, for Philippa in the next few years, when her own sister gave birth to children by the duke. Chaucer's verses hint at past anguishes, in his own household as well as the duke's.

KATHERINE'S CHILDREN AND DESCENDANTS

Katherine's eldest son Thomas Swynford had a career in Lancastrian and royal service. By 1383 he was receiving the large annuity of £40 a year from Gaunt: in March of that year, as a wedding present, the duke granted instead to Thomas and his bride an annuity of 100 marks for their lives.[39] In 1393 Richard II made an equally-matched grant to the couple. When, after Gaunt's death in 1399, Richard confiscated the Lancastrian inheritance in order to prevent the succession to it of the exiled Henry of Bolingbroke, he tried to keep Swynford's loyalty by confirming Gaunt's grant to him and his wife.[40] However, soon after Henry's usurpation of the throne, Swynford, now Henry's retainer, may have carried his zeal for the House of Lancaster to a terrible extreme. In February 1400 the deposed Richard died, opportunely for Henry IV, in his prison in the great Lancastrian fortress at Pontefract (Yorkshire). A well-informed contemporary chronicler, Adam of Usk, says that the forlorn Richard died 'miserably on the last day of February, as he lay in chains... tormented by Sir N. Swinford with starving fare'. Usk was undoubtedly referring to Sir Thomas. If Swynford was widely held to be responsible for the death of an anointed king, that provides one explanation for his failure to attain further eminence.[41]

Following Katherine's marriage in 1396, her Beaufort children were recognised as legitimate by the pope, a legitimation soon confirmed by Act of Parliament. Gaunt and Richard proceeded to exalt them further than any English royal kinsfolk born in bastardy had been since the twelfth century. The eldest of them, John Beaufort (d. 1410) was speedily elevated as earl of Somerset (1397). In the early 1390s he had made his mark as a jousting companion of his half-brother Henry of Bolingbroke and as a crusader in Tunisia, Lithuania and Hungary. Further honoured by Richard with the title of marquis of Dorset, his relations with Henry were soured by his attempt to oppose the latter's invasion of England in 1399, but Dr Michael K. Jones has shown that he soon became one of Henry's most fervent supporters as king. They are close in death: John Beaufort's tomb, with its fine armoured alabaster effigy, is not far from Henry IV's chantry chapel in Canterbury Cathedral.[42] John's filial piety may be expressed in the 'Beaufort Book of Hours', commissioned for himself and his wife. His mother's name-saint is among those who have invocations, with an exquisite illumination of the saint kneeling before her wheel.[43] The Tudor dynasty descended from John Beaufort; in addition, through his daughter Joan's marriage in 1424 to James I, King of Scots, the royal house of Stuart and the present British royal family have descents from Katherine Swynford. So have the dukes of Beaufort, whose dynastic origins trace back to Charles Somerset, an illegitimate great-grandson of John Beaufort.

Katherine's second son, Henry (d. 1447) was the ablest and most distinguished of her sons. Gaunt had the boy's education polished both at Peterhouse, Cambridge, and Queen's College, Oxford. He shamelessly promoted his son in a youthful clerical career. In 1390, when Henry Beaufort was aged about fifteen, he was collated by royal grant to two prebends in Lincoln Cathedral, one of them the most lucrative in the chapter. In 1398 Pope Boniface IX provided him to the see of Lincoln, from which the aged Bishop Buckingham had been pressed into retiring, not without scandal. During the reigns of his kinsmen the Lancastrian kings, Beaufort emerged as a mainstay of their rule both in England and France and as a formidable power in the politics of the Church Universal. He became bishop of Winchester, chancellor of England and a cardinal. He co-operated with German princes in crusading against the heretical Hussite regime in Bohemia. His splendid chantry chapel can be seen in Winchester Cathedral. The 'Beaufort Brethren' still live in the fine collegiate buildings he had erected at the hospital of St Cross, Winchester, for his new foundation of an almshouse 'of noble poverty' (for distressed gentlefolk) alongside the existing charity. They bear witness to the less worldly instincts of a highly political prelate.[44]

Perhaps the most admirable of Katherine's sons was Thomas

Beaufort, duke of Exeter (d. 1426), though to modern ears he sounds somewhat priggish. When he was a young man, in the 1390s, his interest in jousting was encouraged by his half-brother Henry of Bolingbroke; in 1397, soon after his legitimation, he was retained by Richard II with an annuity of 100 marks. He was to be a leading commander in his nephew Henry V's wars in France; Henry, that stern judge of men, in 1422 entrusted the upbringing of his infant son, the future Henry VI, to Duke Thomas. The latter had gained an outstanding reputation as a noble with high standards of Christian conduct. He was conspicuously charitable to the poor and wayfarers. He would not tolerate swearers, liars and tale-bearers in his household. He would not accept gifts or rewards. His puritanism provides a contrast with some of the disordered aspects of his parents' life-styles.[45]

Katherine's youngest child by Gaunt was her daughter, Joan (d. 1440). She is found residing in her father's household in the early 1390s, and so is her husband, Sir Robert Ferers. He died when she was

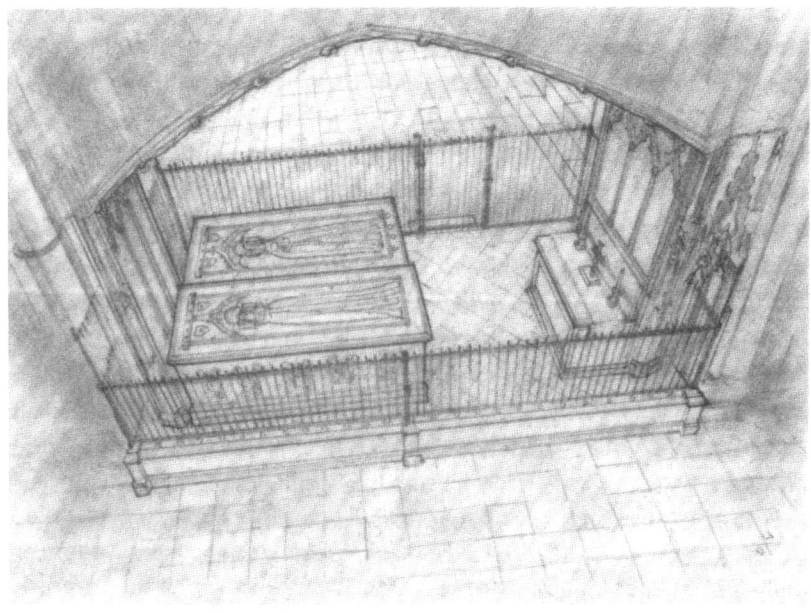

The chapel of the chantry of Katherine Swynford and her daughter Joan:
reconstruction of its original arrangement by David Vale

young and in 1396 she made a far more distinguished marriage, to the head of a leading baronial family, the Nevilles, with whom her father had long had close connections. Her new husband, Ralph lord Neville (d. 1425) was an important magnate in the north of England, soon to be elevated as earl of Westmorland. By him she had thirteen children, with the promotion of whose fortunes she was much preoccupied, especially since the earldom and Neville inheritance descended through Ralph's son by his first wife, Margaret Stafford. Correspondence surviving from Countess Joan's later years of widowhood reveals her as a formidable dowager with a touch of her father's imperiousness.[46] Both her alabaster effigy and that of her connubial predecessor Margaret are to be seen on either side of Ralph's, on the Neville tomb in Staindrop church (County Durham), not far from the family's surviving fourteenth-century residence, magnificent Raby Castle. However, Joan was not prepared to be found at the Last Judgement sharing a tomb with a previous wife, even though the latter did come from one of the most distinguished English families. Instead, she showed her regard for her mother by willing to be buried beside her in the chantry in Lincoln Cathedral.

JOHN OF GAUNT, KATHERINE AND LINCOLNSHIRE
Gaunt's associations with Lincolnshire and with Lincoln Cathedral began in infancy. In 1342, at the age of two, he was granted the earldom of Richmond, the organisation of whose estates in Lincolnshire was centred on Boston. The following year, with his father Edward III and his eldest brother the Black Prince, he visited the cathedral, where he was admitted with them to its confraternity.[47] In 1372 his father's foreign policy necessitated his surrender of the earldom of Richmond, but since 1361, as a result of his first marriage, he had been earl of Lincoln and the possessor of that earldom's extensive possessions in the shire, including the hereditary constableship of Lincoln Castle. In the early 1360s he occasionally stayed at his castle of Bolingbroke, but later in life he preferred, if visiting the shire, to stay at Lincoln itself, though it is not clear whether, on these occasional visits, he stayed in the castle, one of the canons' houses in the close or in one of the merchants' houses. Gaunt

had a special affection for the cathedral and devotion for its patroness, the Virgin Mary. This was to be reflected in the exceptionally lavish bequests which he made to the cathedral of vestments and ecclesiastical furnishings from the chapel of his private household, including an altar which he had purchased abroad whose sculptures were adorned with precious jewels: the altar was valued at over £387.[48] In 1390-1 Gaunt showed a sympathetic bias towards the cathedral chapter in arbitrating long-standing disputes which the canons had with the citizens of Lincoln over the extra-civic jurisdiction claimed for the cathedral close, disputes which paralleled those which Gaunt had with the citizens in his capacity as constable of the castle, over the jurisdiction of the castle's 'liberty', the Bail.[49]

It is possible that Gaunt's first connection with Katherine resulted from his earlier tenure of the earldom of Richmond, for the knightly Swynford family held some of their Lincolnshire property as feudal tenants of the earldom.[50] So it was a natural step for the young Hugh Swynford to seek a career in the service of his overlord and an office for his wife in the household of his lady, if, indeed, the unmarried Katherine, through her father's court connections, had not already been placed with Blanche of Lancaster.[51] Young Katherine Swynford, as a substantial local landowner's wife with exalted connections, was persona grata with the canons of Lincoln. Two of the canons, Thomas de Sutton and John de Warsop, stood godfather to her son Thomas Swynford, when he was christened the day after his birth at Lincoln in the church of St Margaret in the Close. Many years later witnesses recalled the events of that day. John Liminour of Lincoln (presumably a book illuminator) brought two books to the church, one of them a Missal, and sold them to Warsop. The parish clerk testified that he had carried the chrism from the altar to the font, a servant of Sutton's brought fire to light the candle, another man held a basinful of water for the godfathers and godmother to wash in and another a towel for them to dry their hands on. Katherine's chamberlain, Gilbert de Beseby of Lincoln, brought clothes of silk and cloth of gold to the church, presumably in which to wrap the baptised infant.[52]

After Sir Hugh Swynford's death in 1371, Katherine received his manor of Kettlethorpe, not far from Lincoln, as jointure.[53] This was a convenient country retreat for her when she was a ducal governess, for it was not far off the routes taken by the Lancastrian household on its customary travels between the south of England and castles and hunting-lodges in Yorkshire. Katherine may have retired to the obscurity of Kettlethorpe rather than remain amidst the prying eyes of Lincoln whenever her pregnant state in the 1370s threatened to become scandalously evident. It was to Kettlethorpe that Gaunt, when at Heriford in January 1375, directed his receiver of estates in Lincolnshire to send with all possible haste a barrel of the best Gascon wine he could buy, or, if none was available, the best Rhenish.[54] The following July Gaunt ordered that sixty oaks best fitted for construction be selected from his parks at Gringley and Wheatley (Nottinghamshire) and dispatched for building works at Katherine's properties in Kettlethorpe.[55] Gaunt himself stayed there for a few days in 1379.[56] It may have been thither that Katherine vanished during the Peasants' Revolt: compulsorily retired from her post of governess soon afterwards, she may have spent more time there and put some of her considerable wealth into improving the facilities of her estate. In 1383 Katherine received a royal licence to enclose and empark 300 acres within the manor.[57] In front of the present Kettlethorpe Hall (rebuilt more than once since her time) is a large detached stone arch, quite elaborately decorated, dating from the fourteenth century. Today its grandeur appears somewhat out of place: it would be nice to think that it was part of Katherine's building works, and that here we have a memorial to a remarkable lady and her scandalous life.

In advancing age Katherine's health may have suffered from Kettlethorpe's damp situation: its meadow was regularly flooded.[58] In 1386-7 she had recently had repairs done to the Chancery of Lincoln Cathedral, in Minster Yard, which she was renting from the Dean and Chapter; she was doing so in 1391-2.[59] In March 1391 Gaunt had had Gascon wine sent to her by cart from London to Lincoln.[60] It may well have been that the canons leased the Chancery to Katherine as a favour to Gaunt. He had been present in chapter in February 1386 on the occasion when his son, Henry of Bolingbroke, was admitted to the confraternity. Among those admitted with Henry were Katherine's sons John Beaufort and Thomas Swynford and her sister Philippa

Chaucer.[61]

The history and architectural development of the Chancery (11 Minster Yard) were worked out by Dr Kathleen Major in her pamphlet, Minster Yard (1984) and by the joint authors of *The Survey of Ancient Houses in Lincoln*.[62] In 1321 the Chancellor, Anthony Bek, made

an agreement with the Dean and Chapter for the exchange of his house for a more commodious one, which an earlier canon, Thomas de Ashby (d. 1260) had donated to the Chapter for the Fabric Fund. The present front part of the Chancery, as rebuilt c. 1500, occupies the site of what was probably the main part of Ashby's house, of which some vestiges are identifiable. Anthony Bek, however, wanted to have a

View of The Chancery, Lincoln, from the east, as it may have looked at the time of Katherine Swynford

more ambitious residence. He built a new bloc behind and detached from the main part of the earlier house, partly by remodelling an existing back range which extended eastwards along the northern side of the plot, but mainly by the construction of a new hall at ground level, one end of which abutted on to his service offices and private apartments in the older range. Bek's hall was impressive: in 1343 work was done on fourteen new windows in it. Katherine could have lived in the Chancery in some splendour. Bek's hall has long since been demolished, but parts of the adjoining range, much remodelled, remain. Katherine would have recognised the three doorways which led from the service departments (kitchen, buttery and pantry) into the hall, and also, substantially, the chapel upstairs with its fine piscina.

In her second widowhood Katherine returned to live in Minster Yard: in 1400-1 she was the tenant at 'The Priory' (2 Minster Yard) and it was probably there that she died in 1403. Today The Priory is externally nearly all Victorian in appearance, with a few features remaining which were there in Katherine's day. Some fine interior pieces of carved stonework might have been familiar to her.[63] In her later years she may have exercised more staid charms on the canons: one of them, Peter Dalton, Treasurer, left her a silver cup in his will.[64] Shortly before her death, and probably in anticipation of its imminence, she secured from Henry IV half of her annual grant of wine for her son Sir Thomas Swynford.[65] Some bequests which she made show her devotion to the cathedral and its sacred patroness and her gratitude for the kindnesses of the Chapter. The 1536 inventory of the Cathedral Treasury lists luxurious sets of priestly vestments which had belonged to the chapel of her household and which she had donated to the cathedral, many of them decorated in gold and silver thread with her distinctive emblem, the Catherine Wheel.[66]

KATHERINE'S TOMB AND CHANTRY

Katherine received from the Dean and Chapter of Lincoln the great privilege for a lay person of the right to be buried and have a chantry chapel, where masses would be said in perpetuity for her soul, within the choir of the cathedral, on the south side of the sanctuary. Hers is the larger of the two table-tombs (the smaller being that of her daughter Joan) which now lie in line under a canopied fragment of the chantry, on the south side of the presbytery, occupying the western bay of the sanctuary and projecting into the south aisle. The chantry and tombs have been authoritatively studied by John H. Harvey: what follows is based mainly on his work and conclusions.[67]

The arrangement for Katherine to be buried there can be connected with the royal licence of September 1398 for the foundation in the cathedral of a chantry employing two chaplains (to pray for the good estate of the duke and duchess of Lancaster) and for the appropriation to the chantry of the advowson of St Peter's, South Somercotes (Lincolnshire). There appears to have been a considerable delay in completing the foundation,[68] but an altar was certainly in place by Katherine's tomb when her daughter Joan made a refoundation of the chantry in 1437, according to which the welfare and the souls of various Beaufort and Lancastrian kinsmen were to be prayed for.[69]

The tombs today are sadly plain and bereft, having only indents remaining for the brasses which originally adorned them. As for the chantry, little can be accepted as genuine fifteenth-century stonework except the patterned vault and its east and west abutments. The chantry is given an odd appearance by the post-medieval cornice, a replacement doubtless of a soaring original canopy, with niched saints, heraldic panels and richly crocketed finials. One other surviving original feature is the fine wrought-iron grille, carried on a buttressed and moulded stone plinth, which encloses the projection of the chantry into the south aisle.

A drawing of the tombs made by Sir William Dugdale in 1640 shows them conjoined side by side, with canopied brass figures on the tomb tops of mother and daughter in their widows' weeds, and heraldic panels in brass on Joan's tomb. The latter, it is presumed, projected northwards into the sanctuary and then had iron grilles around it extending the area of the chantry. The brasses are likely to have been destroyed and the stonework of the chantry severely damaged in the destruction unleashed on the interior of the cathedral during the Civil War of the seventeenth century. The tombs had been moved to their present position by 1672 and the chantry was probably given its present truncated form in the reconstruction work after the restoration of the monarchy in 1660.

NOTES

1 M. B. Ruud, *Thomas Chaucer* (Minneapolis, 1926), pp.71-3. Unreferenced material is taken from A. Goodman, *John of Gaunt* (1992).

2 M. M. Crow and C. C. Olson (eds), *Chaucer Lifr-Records* (Oxford, 1966), pp. 67-8. The mark was a unit of account equivalent to two-thirds of one pound sterling.

3 *Calendar of Inquisitions Post Mortem* (hereafter *CIPM*), vol. xi, no.197.

4 E. M. Thompson (ed.), *Chronicon Angliae* (Rolls Series, 1874), pp. 195-6.

5 J. R. Lumby (ed.), *Chronicon Henrici Knighton*, vol. ii (Rolls Series, 1895), pp.147-8.

6 M. Bateson (ed.), *Records of the Borough of Leicester*, vol. ii (Cambridge, 1901), pp.155, 171.

7 Lincolnshire Archives Office (hereafter LAO), Bishop Buckingham's Register, fo 26r.

8 *CIPM*, vol. xiii, no.204; S. Armitage-Smith (ed.), *John of Gaunt's Register* (Camden Society 3rd series, 20, 1911; hereafter *JGR 1372-6*), nos. 968-9.

9 *Calendar of Entries in the Papal Registers... Papal Letters*, vol. iv, 1362-1404 (London, 1904), p.545; *JGR 1372-6*, no.181.

10 E. C. Lodge and R. Somerville (ed.), *John of Gaunt's Register, 1379-83* (Camden Society 3rd series, 56, 1937; hereafter *JGR 1379-83*), no.963. For payments to Katherine as governess in 1376-7, Public Record Office (hereafter PRO), DL28/3/1, 3,5.

11 *Papal Letters, 1362-1404*, p.545.

12 Jean Froissart, *Oeuvres*, ed. K. de Lettenhove, vol. xv (Brussels, 1871), p.239.

13 *Calendar of Patent Rolls* (hereafter CPR) *1408-73*, pp.3234.

14 S. Armitage-Smith, *John of Gaunt* (London, 1904), pp.389,462-3.

15 For a list of grants, ibid., p.463.

16 *JGR 1372-6*, no.409.

17 Ibid., nos. 1356-7.

18 Ibid., no.718.

19 *JGR 1379-83*, p.183.

20 *CIPM*, vol. xviii, no.313.

21 V. H. Galbraith (ed.), *The Anonimalle Chronicle* (1970), p.153.

22 Ibid., p.154. For Gaunt's expressions of remorse, see also Knighton, vol. ii, pp. 147-8; Thomas Walsingham, *Historia Anglicana*, ed. H. T. Riley, vol. ii (Rolls Series, 1864), p.43.

23 *JGR 1379-83*, no.984.

24 Ibid., no.1157.

25 Nottinghamshire Record Office, Foljambe of Osberton MSS, DDFJ i 796.

26 J. H. Wylie, *History of England under Henry the Fourth*, vol. iv (London,

27 1898), p.159.

East Sussex Record Office, Glynde Place MS. 3469, Rolls M, A2, A4, A9, B9.

28 H. T. Riley (ed.), *Johannis de Trohelowe... Chronica et Annales* (Rolls Series, 1866),p.188.

29 Froissart, Oeuvres, vol. xv, pp.238-40.

30 L. Douet d'Arcq, *Choix de pi&es inedites relatives au règne de Charles VI*, vol. ii (Paris, 1864), p.276.

31 *CPR 1396-99*, p.76.

32 Ibid., pp.516, 555; PRO, C81/1395/44; cf PRO, 5C8/181/9045.

33 F. Sandford, *A Genealogical History of the Kings of England* (London, 1683), p.248.

34 *JGR 1372-6*, no.409.

35 *Wylie, Henry IV*, vol. iv, pp.162, 165.

36 *CPR 1401-5*, p.218.

37 Lines 70-92.

38 Lines 3172-9.

39 *CPR 1396-99*, p.493.

40 *CPR 1399-1401*, p.295.

41 E. M. Thompson (ed.), *Chronicon Adae de Usk* (London, 1904), pp.42, 198-9 and 199n.

42 M. K. Jones and M. G. Underwood, *The King's Mother: Lady Margaret Beaufort* (Cambridge, 1992), pp.21-3.

43 British Library, Royal MS.2 A XVIII, f 15v, 16r-v.

44 G. L. Harriss, *Cardinal Beaufort* (Oxford, 1988).

45 William Worcestre, *Itineraries*, ed. J. H. Harvey (Oxford, 1969), pp.356-9.

46 R. B. Dobson, *Durham Cathedral Priory 1400-1450* (Cambridge, 1973), p. 187.

47 Crow and Olson, *Chaucer Life-Records*, p.48. The confraternity was a group of benefactors remembered in the prayers of the cathedral community.

48 C. Wordsworth, 'Inventories of Plate', *Archaeologia*, 2nd series, 3 (1892); J. F. Wickenden, '"Joyalx" of John of Gaunt', *Archaeological Journal* 32 (1875); cf LAO, Dean and Chapter MSS, Bj/2/10, fo 12r.

49 Ibid., Bj/2/8, fos 8v, 9r, 10v, 28v,29r; J. W. F. Hill, *Medieval Lincoln* (Cambridge, 1948), pp. 262-8.

50 *CIPM*, vol. xiii, no.204.

51 Hugh Swynford was intending to go in Gaunt's military retinue to Aquitaine in 1366, and, if he went, is likely to have taken part with his lord in the Black Prince's Castilian campaign of 1367 (*Foedera, Conventiones, Litterae...* [etc.J, ed. A. Clarke *et al.* (4 vols, London, 1816-69), vol. iii, Pt ii, p.812).

52 *CIPM*, vol. xvii, no.576. The proof of age was taken in 1394 and the witnesses dated the birth to 1373. Other evidence suggests that Thomas was born before that year.

53 *Calendar of Close Rolls 1369-74*, p.388.

54 *JGR 1372-6*, no.1608.

55 Ibid., no.1711.

56 *JGR 1379-83*, nos. 108-115.

57 *CPR 1381-5*, p.317. For a grant to Katherine by Henry son of John de Fenton of tenements in Kettlethorpe and its appurtenances (1386), see LAO, Amcotts VI/A/22/2.

58 *CIPM*, vol. XI, no.197.

59 S. Jones, K. Major and J. Varley, *The Survey of Ancient Houses in Lincoln*, fasc. i (Lincoln Civic Trust, 1984), pp.52-3. I owe thanks for this reference to Dr Nicholas Bennett.

60 PRO, DL28/3/2, 25.

61 Crow and Olson, *Chaucer Life-Records*, pp.91-2.

62 Jones, *Ancient Houses*, pp.52-3. See also N. Pevsner and J. Harris, *The Buildings of England: Lincolnshire* (London, 1964), pp. 137-8.

63 Jones, *Ancient Houses*, pp.25, 32; Pevsner and Harris, p.138.

64 A. Gibbons (ed.), *Early Lincoln Wills* (Lincoln, 1888), pp. 96-8.

65 *CPR 1401-5*, p.218.

66 Wordsworth, 'Inventories', pp.23-4.

67 J. H. Harvey, *Catherine Swynford's Chantry* (Lincoln Minster Pamphlets, 2nd series, no.6).

68 Wickenden, '"Joyalx"', pp.319, 321-5. Gaunt's executors acknowledged their failure to complete the chantry foundations devised by him in indentures made with the Dean and Chapter dated 1400, 1402 and 1413.

69 *CPR 1436-42*, p.137.